PASTA

by Gretchen Will Mayo

Reading consultant: Susan Nations, M.Ed., author/literacy coach/consultant

WEEKLY WR READER®
EARLY LEARNING LIBRARY

Please visit our web site at: www.earlyliteracy.cc
For a free color catalog describing Weekly Reader® Early Learning Library's
list of high-quality books, call 1-877-445-5824 (USA) or 1-800-387-3178 (Canada).
Weekly Reader® Early Learning Library's fax: (414) 336-0164.

Library of Congress Cataloging-in-Publication Data available upon request from publisher.
Fax (414) 336-0157 for the attention of the Publishing Records Department.

ISBN 0-8368-4069-0 (lib. bdg.)
ISBN 0-8368-4076-3 (softcover)

This edition first published in 2004 by
Weekly Reader® Early Learning Library
330 West Olive Street, Suite 100
Milwaukee, WI 53212 USA

Copyright © 2004 by Weekly Reader® Early Learning Library

Editor: JoAnn Early Macken
Art direction, cover and layout design: Tammy Gruenewald
Photo research: Diane Laska-Swanke
Photographer: Gregg Andersen

Printed in the United States of America

1 2 3 4 5 6 7 8 9 08 07 06 05 04

Table of Contents

Pasta can be made in many tasty ways.

Simple and Tasty

Pasta is eaten in many ways. It can be covered with tomato sauce. It can be served with cheese or vegetables. It can appear in hot dishes or salads. Sometimes it even acts as dessert.

The recipe for pasta is simple. Flour, water, and salt are the only ingredients. Sauces turn pasta into a tasty meal.

Pasta has only three ingredients.

Different spices change the taste of noodles.

Making Pasta

Pasta is an Italian word. It means pieces of dough that are boiled, not baked. Many people around the world eat pasta. Koreans make cold noodle soup. People in China stir-fry wheat noodles in lo mein. Kugel is a Jewish sweet noodle dish.

Pasta can be made with rice flour or wheat flour. Rice noodles are white. They are most often used in Asian dishes. Cooks mix them with vegetables, nuts, and sauces.

Pasta is perfect with vegetables.

A farmer inspects wheat grains.

Wheat flour is used in the most popular American pastas. The best flour keeps its shape when it is cooked. Any pasta turns flabby if it is boiled too long.

All pasta making begins with flour. Home cooks buy it in bags. Pasta factories order a truckload or railroad car full of flour. A special vacuum hose sucks the flour into bins inside the factory.

A railroad car brings wheat flour into a factory.

A worker empties flour into a mixing tub.

The flour is mixed with water to form dough.
In a pasta factory, the dough is mixed in huge
tubs. Dried vegetables may be added to the
dough. Pepper, lemon, or other flavors might
be mixed in, too.

Next, the dough moves to pressing machines. It is kneaded, or squeezed, until it is firm. When the dough is just right, it is ready to be shaped.

A machine kneads the pasta dough.

Eggs are used in some pasta recipes.

Pasta Shapes

Noodles are the simplest pasta to make in the
factory or at home. Eggs or egg yolks are usually
added to the dough. The dough is rolled into
sheets. The sheets are cut into long, thin strips.
At the factory, a machine cuts the noodle strips to
the right width and length.

Spaghetti is the best-loved pasta in the United States. It does not contain eggs. Spaghetti is an Italian word. It means "little strings." Thinner strings of pasta are called vermicelli. It means "little worms." The thinnest pasta is called angel hair.

Spaghetti, vermicelli, and angel hair
are made from pasta dough.

Spaghetti dough is forced through a die.

Spaghetti is long and thin. It is not made the same way as noodles. It is extruded, or forced through a die. A die is a large metal disk with holes in it.

The holes in a die shape the dough. Star holes make star-shaped pasta. Round holes make rods like spaghetti.

A die with round holes makes pasta with a round shape.

Special dies make macaroni.

A steel pin can be placed in the center of each die hole. Then the dough comes out as a tube. Macaroni is a tube. A special kind of pin makes the dough curl. Then it is cut with a knife.

Bow ties are the hardest pasta shapes to make. They are stamped out of flat sheets of dough. At the same time, the bows are pinched in the middle.

Bow tie pasta dresses up a meal.

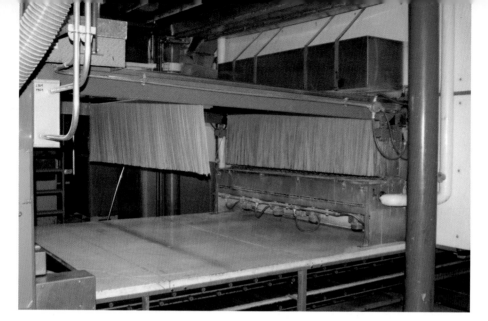

Strips of noodles are air dried.

Pasta must be dried with care. If it dries too quickly, it will break easily. If it dries too slowly, it might spoil. In the factory, hot, moist air dries the pasta.

The factory packages the pasta. It is put in bright boxes or clear bags. A measured amount is dropped into each package. Then the pasta is shipped away in cartons.

A worker inspects filled spaghetti packages.

Try to eat grains at every meal.

Pasta Choices

Pasta is one of the grain foods on the food pyramid. We need to eat six servings of grain foods a day.

You can choose from dozens of kinds of pasta.
Which kind do you like best?

Curly or straight, pasta is a good food choice.

Glossary

Asian — related to Asia or its people

boiled — cooked in bubbling hot and steaming liquid

disk — a thin, flat object with a circular shape

extruded — forced through a hole or holes

flabby — limp, not firm

ingredients — parts that make up a mixture

kneaded — worked and mixed by folding, pressing, and stretching

sauce — a liquid mixture served with another food

stir-fry — to mix while cooking in oil

For More Information

Books

Egan, Robert. *From Wheat to Pasta*. NY: Children's Press, 1997.

Julius, Jennifer. *I Like Pasta. Good Food* Series. NY: Children's Press, 2001.

Sayre, April Pulley. *Noodle Man: The Pasta Superhero*. NY: Orchard Books, 2002.

Spilsbury, Louise. *Pasta. Food* Series. Chicago: Heinemann Library, 2001.

Web Sites

Grains Nutrition Information Center Photos
www.wheatfoods.org/photos/pasta.html
Great pictures of many kinds of pasta eaten around the world

Pasta Shapes
www.ilovepasta.org/shapes.html
A chart of different pastas with information about their uses

Wheat Mania! All about wheat
www.wheatmania.com/allaboutwheat/wheatfacts/wheatkernel.htm
See a grain of wheat up close and learn about its parts

Index

About the Author

Gretchen Will Mayo likes to be creative with her favorite foods. In her kitchen, broccoli and corn are mixed with oranges to make a salad. She sprinkles granola on applesauce. She blends yogurt with orange juice and bananas. She experiments with different pasta sauces. When she isn't eating, Ms. Mayo writes stories and books for young people like you. She is also a teacher and illustrator. She lives in Wisconsin with her husband, Tom, who makes delicious soups. They have three adult daughters.